UNDERSTANDING DEPRESSION THROUGH CLINICAL HYPNOSIS

(With a Case History report)

Shiva Swati

ISBN: 9781791536374

Dedication

This book is dedicated to helping Earth clear negative energy by erasing of hypocrisy and through upliftment of positivity in humanity in alignment with the energies of ascension in the NEW AGE aiming at defeating energies of depression by freeing souls from pressure of the vacuum cult.

Table of Contents

Chapter 1- Depression: The Alternative Ascension Perspective

"Overcoming Depression leads to ascension of average positive frequency, soul evolution, a healthier mind & more balanced ambitions, when the pressures of hypocrisy or metaphoric gas, are released with a zeal for developing optimism, positive thinking , hope , satisfaction and spiritually aligned meditative abilities "

Depression is spreading like rapid fire these days. Problems appear to rise when people start talking about them whereas they may have been dormant through centuries. However, problems can also literally increase when there is excessive accumulation of trauma in the mass consciousness and immunity falls for society, as a whole; thus , leading to each falling backwards. This analogy is similar to pollution of air. When there is too much pollution, breathing of each is negatively affected. Similarly, when there is too much hypocrisy in society, well-being of each thinking person is negatively affected.

While rational logic can be devised on theoretical layers and medicines prescribed by research on chemical grounds, there is much need to understand the energy underlying the spread of depression to check its exponential growth. Usually, depression is caused due to the circumstances of a person which are affected by a multitude of factors that cannot be controlled as chemical reactions can be. However, the circumstances can be deciphered through methods like hypnotherapy so that the person can view his or her own self –deception and heal.

The healing of depression requires release of suppressed tension by either changing the circumstances or viewing the self from a detached, observer's perspective. Depression goes into the background when illusions of a perfect world , a perfect education scenario, a perfect self , a perfect marriage and a perfect job break while imperfections are accepted as a natural norm of life, such that *'freedom to be naturally different'* replaces chains of *'why can I not be conventionally perfect '*,in the mind.

Depression is largely a result of self- deception .You become depressed when you feel helpless because things are not as you believe they should be and you cannot do anything about the situation.

For example, depression in school children can be traced to inadequate sleep patterns, trust being broken repeatedly, unfair criticism, unnecessary performance expectations and excessive pressure on the child's mind to fit into success norms of the world which have been proven to have failed in creating satisfaction or happiness.

Children feel insecure and are over stressed often due to irregular family timings or an aggressive family atmosphere. While preaching discipline to the young minds, at a theoretical level, adults' own practice does not match the preaching, leaving kids confused and sad. In practice, adults in a modern life style have irregular timings and aggressive relationships since everyone is running the rat race along with seeking some semblance of fun, with hardly any time left for harmonizing the body, health and inner space. Last priority effort is invested on stress release as the traditional concept of fun is connected with rebelling secretly while compromising conventionally with the hypocrisy in which you are expected to fit in. Thus, there is dancing, alcoholism, partying, excessive eating, socializing in clubs, pubs or unwinding in discotheques which creates even more stress once layers of self- deception creep up in the subconscious mind, leading to seeds of depression.

A healthy mind is an outcome of making a priority to invest some time towards being in peace in free, inner space where there is no pressure to perform in any manner, not even by the clothes you wear or by the ways you choose to differ from others' thinking; where you have time to just be and contemplate on your positive energies. Feelings of peace and inner space help in healing depression by opening up illusory chains tying up traditional beliefs in the mind.

However, contrary to this need for inner peace, adult relaxation in today's world is centred around insisting on flamboyant fun, pretending happiness where none exists in everyday life, drinking alcohol or taking drugs to insist that there is no need for deeper change and their illusions of a magnificent world are real, competitive lies , deceit and image keeping.

However, young adults or teenagers find it difficult to understand this hypocrisy as it onsets suddenly. A growing up child can feel disillusioned and collapse with the energy of surface lies as a fish without stability when the water is found dirty and infected with the virus of cheating.

It is likewise, often observed that depression sets in after marriage when love gets betrayed by the need to follow social norms; depression sets in with a new job when you don't get a chance to professionally grow as you seek; depression sets in while doing social service where you cannot change people's mind-sets whether they are victims or abusers, depression sets in while combating a non- curable physical disease, depression sets in new mothers by constantly staying awake with new-borns without adequate sympathy & support, etc.. .All situations which create depression cannot pass away. Some situations can be changed with enforcing self- understanding while other circumstances have to be accepted without feeling helpless or hopeless, as evolving soul lessons for learning detachment.

Overcoming depression as a mass consciousness necessitates a complete change of the education system where you are taught emotional management from school so that you can learn how to remove negative energy from your mind on a regular basis before it camouflages in as negative pressure that creates disease or depression.

One of the simplest methods of help which can be presently given by schools can be more time to sleep by keeping flexible timings or afternoon shifts for children who prefer sleeping late; as sleeping is at least one form of rest where you are free of pressure. Extra sleeping time can help children have inner space to contemplate and resolve their issues without feeling pressured by studies or sports or other performances. Everyone does not work well with deadlines and the flexibility to work without strict time schedules needs to exist for several children who like to understand concepts with real-life applications, than memorize them to pass grades.

Extra sleeping time also helps to improve memory as it clears up suppressed cobwebs in the mind. You need to be alone for about two or three hours every day other than the regular 8 sleeping hours , to self-reflect and release the energy of sadness or abuses which you encounter in everyday life. You can sit in a restful state to just focus on your breathing or meditate on feeling yourself as an energy radiating being, if you don't get sleep in the extra two hours allotted to you to de-stress.

You need to prioritize free time to be in your private space instead of watching television or socializing which may increase your tension. Being alone and non- judged would help you calm down your nerves and balance your hormones. By calming down your nerves, you will have time to unravel your inner intelligence which is needed to improve your mind power and health.

Extra rest or meditation time where you can be away from everyday worries ,thoughtless or day dreaming , improves quality work performance and reduces the need for active fun which is stress creating . Whether you dance or paint or sing or study to de-stress, simultaneously ,being alone in a positive state of mind helps. Taking idle time, whether to sleep or meditate, would improve your performance more than slogging out endlessly. Performance improves through rest as has been proved by research, as it leads to an active release of positive neural impulses over stressed, negative hormones.

Sleep time is especially required by patients of depression to feel balanced. If pressurized continuously, they become suicidal. Depressed patients need hours of thoughtlessness so that the mind rises from negative thinking to feeling neutral or detached. Positive thinking is possible only after neutral states of mind are activated and maintained.

Hence, flexible timings and less pressure on performing need to be implemented so that children and adults feel less like robots and more humanly alive .

Depression heals when you can determinedly focus on releasing positive hormones in the mind to dissolve the negative hormones which have created depression... as by meditating, smiling or day dreaming of happy moments, while just being idle. Metaphorically, you are never idle as your mind is always working just as a saint is never idle . But allowing the mind to work without having to meet other people's demands is necessary to connect to God's life force within the body and energize inner satisfaction...

Where circumstances are challenging and there are incidents of molestation, rape, excessive beating or verbal abuse, lowering of self- esteem, poverty etc. there is a need to address these situations at an emotional level for the soul to heal.

Adult depression is much more deep-rooted and takes much more emotional work to heal. Medicines often make the depressed person sleepy because they aim at calming down the negative hormones by releasing positive hormones in the mind. However, if the person's rate of thinking negative thoughts /negative feelings is higher than the rate at which the medicines produce positive feelings and positive hormones, the medicines fail to help. All medicines increase sleep as sleeping helps the person since ideally, she or he does not think negative thoughts at the time of sleeping.

Depression is the opposite frequency of ascension of the soul. It always leads to a questioning of the* status quo. You question your own beliefs, values and the structure of happiness that is held as correct in society. Overtime, you start feeling bound by chains as you realize that everything that is being held as being good in society is not always appropriate... Subsequently, if *you can believe that your chains are only in the mind, you can rise above their mental

hold. By uplifting your spirit ,you move towards soul ascension, a healthier body and a more peaceful mind, wherein you care more about your own karmic choices and feel less helpless about being unable to pacify other people's demands.

By realizing that you are healthy and active when you are not depressed, you can make efforts to be less depressed by understanding and pursuing what makes you happy as against following what others think should make you happy. By thinking independently, you would uplift your mind-set over other people's expectations from you to fulfil your own definitions of contentment. You would be able to detach from worries about survival or money or about how they think or perceive your decisions. You would also detach from the primitive ape man's mind conditioning which revolved around insecurity, fear and survival as that carries over subconsciously unless deliberately deconditioned..

Overtime, as you find what makes you happy by ignoring what makes other people unhappy about you, you would discover that other people's sadness or happiness is not directly connected to you being good or bad but continues to exist irrespective of whether you are nice or selfish in their perspective. You would detach and be more positive overtime as you continue to be independent of others' sorrows or expectations as other people's needs or sorrows are their own soul tests which you cannot pass for them. Overcoming their own sadness without forcing others to be sad would help in their karmic evolution just as overcoming your depression would help in your soul ascension towards a better quality of emotional satisfaction....

The example case history of depression in chapter 2 depicts how medicines to heal depression failed as the trauma had to be understood before it could be released. While medicines can complement emotional healing, they cannot substitute subconscious analysis or healing of trauma in the soul. Depression needs a holistic approach. The person remains suppressed internally till s/he is made aware of which thought is causing depression and where the thought maybe coming from, and if certain changes in choices of life have to be made in order to free the mind from falling again and again into depression.

Chapter 2- HYPNOSIS as a TOOL OF TREATMENT

" Allowing yourself to access your suppressed trauma in hypnosis helps you understand your inner needs as a rational being seeking help to save the lights of the inner self from drowning in flooding waters of sorrow"

Clinical Hypnosis is a guided healing methodology. It can be used clinically for treatment of chronic problems through a process called hypnotherapy. Hypnotherapy can be applied only if the person is willing by himself or herself to heal i.e. if s/h recognizes that there is a problem which needs to be addressed within the self. Thus, it successfully caters to people who are willing to develop an awareness of negative thinking in the self with the intention of overcoming it and changing to being positive. Hypnosis cannot work if you refuse to willingly participate in the guided process of accessing your subconscious mind.

Unlike medication or magic, clinical hypnosis cannot be applied unless the person understands his role in his own healing than being just a victim of circumstances. Hypnosis only changes the self and not the others involved. Hypnosis works for those who take responsibility to heal with guided help and not for those who do not accept that any problem exists within the self, and only blame others, like the government or their circumstances .(Though, the government or the circumstances may be at fault but, instead of blaming the external circumstances ,which is akin metaphorically to the primitive man blaming the rain for draught ,a qualitatively better system of contributing to a positive world can be developed through releasing past traumatic memories i.e. negative energy of the mind and freeing inner space for radiating out positive, constructive energy with more confidence .)

Hypnosis does not work by deception or force as it heals by changing the mind's core habit of negative thinking to positive over a period of time of focused effort.

What is Hypnosis?

Hypnosis is a state of mind where the brain waves are slowed down so that attention can be focused more on a single activity, wherein critical judgment is partially suspended and peripheral awareness is diminished. The client has to be a willing participant as healing does not produce long term benefits, if enforced.

Hypnosis has been found to be useful for improving concentration in adolescents and adult, for removing fears and phobias, for healing anxieties and depressions, for conflict integration and for the treatment of diseases controlled by the autonomic nervous system like asthma, diabetes, indigestion, spondylitis etc.

History of Hypnosis

Hypnosis as is used today is called Clinical Hypnosis which is not the same as mesmerism. Clinical Hypnosis was developed by Dr. James Braid in 1840, who was a British physician. The state of hypnosis is different from mesmerism or a non-thinking, deep trance state. The mesmerized trance state is more like a delta state where the person is in deep sleep and does not remember anything upon awakening.

Under clinical hypnosis, the person remains awake and in self-control while the mind is induced into a state of peaceful calmness away from the hustle of a busy life.

Hypnosis vs. Mesmerism

Hypnosis was first explored by Franz Mesmer. He introduced the concept of Animal Magnetism. Mesmer believed that he had the power to magnetize people under his control. He published his theories of mesmerism in 1765. Most people thought it was black magic or witch-craft.

Clinical hypnosis is the reverse of mesmerism as you are put more in command of your life by a connection to your subconscious self. When you are using hypnosis for healing, you feel safe as your conscience cannot be tampered with, unlike in mesmerism where you are used as a puppet and forget everything upon waking up.

The mesmerized state can be used against the person's free will to harm his/her body or self -interest by using him like a toy under command of the magician. On the other hand, hypnosis puts responsibility of healing on the person by his active participation in treatment of the self. Treatment through hypnotherapy usually leads to an involuntary change in beliefs and values which govern the client's choices of thinking in everyday life.

Attributes Required for the Hypnotic Process

- Hypnosis works on the principle that when the brain waves slow down, the person does more focused mind work than when he is anxious or restless.

The effectiveness of Hypnotherapy depends on the following attributes:

Absorption or Receptivity – the client has to trust the process. S/he has to be willing to do the relaxation exercises to calm the mind and be willing to go into the semi-trance state which the process and the therapist facilitate. If a client mocks or laughs or questions continuously during the induction, the calming, neutral state of hypnosis cannot be activated.

Dissociation-The client has to be willing to detach from his rational, conscious mind activity and allow the subconscious mind to take over as is facilitated by the hypnotic process.

Suggestibility – The client should be willing to imagine. The subconscious mind speaks through pictures, films, colours and symbols. The better the client is at thinking in abstract terms, the easier becomes the treatment under hypnosis.

Dr. Kappas, a renowned hypnotherapist, found that people are influenced by suggestions given in the Hypnotic state, only after the suggestions are accepted by the conscious mind, and not if the suggestions are given in mesmerized state of absent recall.

E.g. If you want to exercise and are unable to get yourself to do it, hypnosis can help you get in a routine of exercising but it will work only if you are willing to exercise at the conscious level. If your values and beliefs contradict the concept of slimming down at the conscious level, the suggestion given under hypnosis will not work.

The process of clinical hypnosis uses a meditative trance to quieten the mind chatter. The person remains in control when the suggestions are given. Healing works only if the person agrees with the process and allows the healing to take place.

On observing several subjects, it was realized by medical practitioners that in a pain state, the subjects were more easily influenced to heal the self by verbal suggestions given in semi-hypnosis than if the suggestions were given in waking state. The subject was influenced to the point of controlling many of his involuntary movements. Since then, clinical hypnosis has been used for healing purposes. It was extensively used on war victims in World War 1 and 2.

- **In 1950`s, Clinical Hypnosis was recognized by the American medical association as a scientific practice.**

Hypnosis Helps To Heal Mental and Physical Disorders Minimizing Medication

Clinical Hypnosis helps to heal mental disorders and physical diseases without using medicines or by minimizing the use of medication.

Clinical Hypnosis works by inducing the brain to move at a slower pace than usual, which gives the mind time for review and change rigid patterns of thinking.

The brain frequencies are lowered under hypnosis, than under a conscious, awake state of mind so that the person has time to observe his own life as an observer and decide whether his choices on internal dialogue are rational or irrational.

There are four types of brain frequencies - beta (>14 cycles /second), alpha (7-14 cycles/second), theta (4-7 cycles /second), delta (< 4 cycles/second).In a conscious state, you are in beta. Thousands of thoughts are passing your minds every second. In alpha; you are in a sleep like state, as in just before going to sleep. You are calm and relaxed but alert of surroundings. In theta, you are in a dream state. It is a state when you can see lucid dreams also. You are aware of your surroundings but less than in alpha. In Delta, you are in deep sleep. There is no awareness of surroundings.

Hypnosis Speeds up Inner Change required for Treatment

Hypnosis speeds up the change process because suggestions for inner change have to be given when the person is calm and the suggestions are absorbed by the subconscious mind. If the suggestion is given when the conscious mind is active and alert, (the Beta State of mind) it brings up too many doubts and arguments which make change appear impossible. If the same suggestions are given again and again, inner resistance creates psychological walls of non-acceptance which make the process of change even more difficult.

If the suggestion is given when a person is asleep as in Delta state of mind, it is often clouded by other dreams or rejected as hallucination. Some people try to pass ideas through dream telepathy which does not work much to bring about motivation for inner change. Commanding the subconscious mind without acknowledgement by the logical mind does not help in creating a motivational need for changing the mindset to more positive on a routine basis

Dialogue between the Conscious and Subconscious Mind

The purpose of using Clinical Hypnosis is to be able to access the conscious mind and the subconscious mind simultaneously such that a dialogue can be created between the person and his/her inner self. A consensus between the soul and the body is achieved by accessing both states of mind at the same time.

Under clinical hypnosis, you view how your body stores memories, how your choices affect your hormonal balance and how negative thinking literally creates diseases in your body. The process is designed such that you remain alert and can remember everything upon recalling the session. You stay focused mentally throughout the session albeit in a calm, less restless, more alert, focused state.

For the power of hypnosis to work most effectively, the person must stay awake. It is only when the conscious mind is awake and receiving information that the information can slip into the subconscious.

Treatment works more when the responsibility of healing is put on the patient by showing alternative thinking patterns under hypnosis.

The Concept Underlying Subconscious Healing Through Hypnosis

The subconscious mind cannot distinguish between imagination and reality as it reads only energies.

The world does not directly affect the brain except through neural impulses. An idea is impacted on the subconscious mind through the internal stimuli produced by action of the sensory organs and the subsequent energy release along with release of neural, electric impulses in the brain and simultaneous hormonal release. In response to the stimuli, an emotion is created. The subconscious mind responds to the emotion. Where there is no color, or sound or feel or emotion created, there is no information internalized by the subconscious mind.

The subconscious mind takes an emotion to be real whether it is imagined or real in the world. Hence, healing works on the principle that for the subconscious mind, an imagined emotion is real even, if it is mentally created because it releases the same amount of energy, electric impulses and hormones as if it were real. The more intensely the emotions are imagined, the more real it seems to the subconscious mind.

For example, if you do not want to get angry over minor things, you can practice other choices of internal response through self-hypnosis. The programmed reaction can replace the automated reaction in the brain. Whatever reaction you create in your mind will be taken as direction by your subconscious mind and your future impulses will be based on the programmed reaction.

To reprogram your automatic reactions, you have to practice mentally, the new mental programs repetitively so that the old reactions are replaced with consistent substitution over a period of time. You can use self -hypnosis after a clinical hypnosis session or without it to program your mind to a new habit of thinking, depending on the intensity of your problem. You have to relive the same situation in your mind while in a calm or self-hypnotic trance and reframe your reactions.

Programming your Own Mind through Self Hypnosis

Self Hypnosis can be used for programming your own mind and learning the process of hypnotic induction.

The first step towards induction is to be in a calm , semi drowsy state of mind where you are awake but less restless. A naturally occurring hypnotic state is when you are about to sleep or when you get up early morning .Self Hypnosis works most when practiced on self at night or early morning or when you are in a semi drowsy state .

For example, to be less angry in your reactions, you may practice a scenario where you are calm given the same stimulus as if it does not push your anger buttons. You can create a scenario of how you want to behave without being angry and practice the alternative responses at night before sleeping and whenever you think of the memory. The more you break your memory circuits through alternate ,positive or neutral, neurological responses, the more your internal neurological circuits will stop creating angry impulses in that situation. The effect will overtime spread to other reactions and you will find yourself calmer overall just by practicing an alternative way to be in your mind.

The more you work at your reactions in your imagination, the more your rationally ordained negative energy will weaken and the less it will harm you . If you do this response programming consistently, every night, you are effectively changing the set of instructions you give to your subconscious mind. Overtime, the subconscious mind will stop creating stress hormones, which   make you have health problems. You will feel more at peace within and the positive hormones released will improve your health . Your autonomic nervous system will not create psychosomatic diseases (e.g. Indigestion, asthma, cancer et.) in your body which occur due to stored anger.

Other Methods of Anger Management through Self Hypnosis (Shielding, detachment etc.)

A Clinical Therapy session of Hypnosis uses about 7 to 11 inductions on after another to get the client into a calm state during daytime. Self -Hypnosis requires about one induction technique, meditation or a natural semi drowsy state.

A relaxed mental state akin to hypnosis can be self-created by using a time where you are already semi drowsy.

Continuing on the same example of reducing angry reactions: The principle in anger management is to be aware that you heal yourself when you develop immunity to an emotional energy attack, subconsciously so that inner feelings of anger are not created.

To develop Immunity regularly, release stress - To release stress, before sleeping at night, feel yourself being washed by a shower of white light which takes away excessive storage of negative energy as bathing takes away negative energy. Feel yourself washed and calm. This will overnight reduce storage of anger in your subconscious mind.

To feel calm, you can count yourself slowly down from 25 to 0. Sit on a chair or lie down and keep focusing upwards. As you focus upwards, start counting backwards from 25 to 0. At 25, allow your mind to be silent and relaxed for a minute. Then, visualize the healing you wish to experience as happening in the current moment. A script of self - hypnosis is given in the appendix.

The backward count works as Step 1 of hypnotic induction. This will get you to an alpha level in the mind.

In alpha stet of mind, you can practice responding in a way which does not create stress in you:

For example:

Shielding - you may choose being immune to the stress creating situation in your imagination by imagining it as rain falling over you while holding an umbrella. The abuses fall as rain but you don't get hit by the energy as you have an imagined umbrella on your head. See yourself calm and unaffected after the rain stops or abuses stop.

Detachment - you may choose ignoring the situation as insignificant by imagining yourself much bigger than the abuser. You can imagine the size of the abuser as a child and practice not losing your temper or you can imagine yourself in the situations as an elephant and the abuser as a rat and thus be able to ignore him or her.

Observer/Mirror method – You may imagine the situation which happened as happening on a television or in a mirror and view it as an observer. Then you can program your reactions to get desired results on the television screen.

Changes will not happen overnight but you will find a significant difference in one to six months. Additional therapies maybe added to complement the process of self-healing.

Chapter 3

Case History – Hypnotherapy with Inner Child Healing

"........ so eager to fly but the wings were soiled. She had to heal before she could go high"

Name	Lavanya Kautilya
Age	40.5 years
Relationship Status	Single, Independent
Education	Ph.D.
Profession	Research Director
Income Group	Higher Middle Class
Family	
	Father expired, mother is retired & lives in an ashram ;both parents were working

and were conventionally
successful when active

Problem from the Perspective of Soul, Mind and Body

Body - Fatigue, Exhaustion, Collapse, Excessive Sleepiness

Mind - Does not feel interested in regular life routines,
Depression

Soul and life force - Low frequency energy rotation, Feelings
of lack of alignment

Inductions used

1. Hypnotherapy Induction for Relaxation
2. Aura Cleansing
3. Chakra Cleansing
4. Progressive Relaxation
5. Stress Release Process
6. Muscle Relaxation
7. Eye Catalepsy
8. Grounding
9. Going down the 20 Stairs

Therapies Used

1. Observation Method of Hypnotherapy
2. Neuro - Linguistic Programming
3. Energy Cord Cutting
4. Energy Shower Healing
5. Inner Child Healing
6. Electric Violet Flame Healing
7. Integration of Soul Fragments

Start of The Session

Lavanya took a session to overcome the extreme depression that she had again been feeling since 6 weeks.

During this phase, she did not want to go out of the house. She wanted to sleep the whole day and did not feel interested in doing anything. Normal daily routine of bathing, cooking etc. was difficult for her. She was in melancholy. There was no particular trigger.

Depression was created in her body, mind and soul. By probing, two triggers could be established which could have led to the depression in her body and mind.

Her body was overworked by normal health standards as she had always been on the move since an year. She slept four hours in a day. A normal person sleeps 7-8 hours a day. A very hectic schedule can overtime lead to a complete collapse as an overworked car. Especially as ageing starts, there is more need to take individual space & time to clear the negative energies picked up during empathy calling in everyday life. Lavanya was always on the move and did not take any time to rest and be calm on a daily basis. Depression can be used as a method to be calm and recoup energies in the body, devised by the subconscious mind when the conscious, rational mind refuses to rest, otherwise.

Trigger for the mind to go into giving up on fighting with gravitational energies, as happens in depression, was a recent betrayal felt by the subconscious mind as backstabbing. Lavanya had felt betrayed by her office boss who was trying to appropriate her work as his own. She had had a similar encounter with him in the past but had overcome the pain since; as he had been behaving especially nice after that. However, once she started trusting him again, he again backstabbed her suddenly and she felt killed in spirit. These words denoting feelings felt at a silent level are important as the subconscious mind takes the emotions suppressed but focused upon, as transferred data. Feeling suppressed forcibly is metaphorically the same energy circuit as being killed as the same emotions are triggered in a milder degree. Thus, with these two triggers, it was found that the body was exhausted and the mind felt betrayed, simultaneously. The doubling of exhaustion led to a sudden collapse in flow of the frequency of life force energy.

 Depression is akin to death for the soul and hence-forth, her body started showing symptoms of depression. She went to meet a doctor and was again diagnosed with clinical depression 5 weeks ago.

She did not take any medication as prescribed by the doctor as she had experienced addiction towards a depressive tablet (Valium) one year back, and had been hospitalized because of taking excessive dosage of Valium. She had fainted and was in ICU for five days. She had no recollection of those five days when she was hospitalized. Hence, she did not want to risk taking the tablets again.

However, there were deeper needs of healing required by her soul as was discovered once she went into the hypnotic trance.

While inducing Lavanya, I gave her the suggestions that she would remember everything after the session though her conscious mind would stay awake and not doubt her or block her subconscious mind from speaking abstractedly. The subconscious mind can only speak in feelings or show pictures of energy in motion. The thoughts suppressed are denoted by the emotional content expressed through pictures and tears. The conscious mind and the subconscious mind are connected through the hypnotherapy session with the intent that the conscious mind understands its subconscious needs and can address them in the future by changing its daily habits of thinking, being or working. Healing takes time as the conscious mind takes time to change its habits of negative thinking and become positive.

Hence, she was guided into trance with staying awake.

As soon as she started walking down the 20 steps staircase which led to a metaphoric representation of her own body, there was a sudden tremor like someone pushing her spirit away, as if she was being blocked from entering her own body. An energy which was black in colour was pushing her away and trying to throw her off. She suddenly revolted as in fear of a ghost and tremors appeared on her face.

I gave her support to send the black energy away by using the electric violet flame. I also asked her to imagine two men in white who looked like the police force to take the energy away and put it in a glass bottle. This imagination helped her be back in control and enter her own sprit body without being pushed by the other evil spirit which was dark and venomous.

The Fourth Inner Child Healing Session

Upon moving down into her subconscious energy field, she was directed to be an observer and visualize a film as on T.V., which showed her who the black energy was and how old she was when she had experienced this fear in her life in real. In the film, she saw herself as a five-year-old sitting in her father's lap. The black energy was in her father. (Her father had died sometime back but she had regrets that he had died suddenly and she could not have a confrontation with him before his death. He had been an alcoholic, abusive, generally ungrateful, venomous and flirtatious.)

The subconscious mind brought up the confrontation through pictorial feelings portrayed as a live film. She saw that the father was drinking, and they were watching a film (GONE WITH THE WIND). He was drinking alcohol and ranting. He was holding her very tightly in a way which was non-fatherly. He kept saying '*I love you*' to her again in a manner which was non fatherly. The energy was as if he was talking to his lover. She was very scared but could not get away. He was fondling her oddly. She could feel his penis touching her and she hated it. She was feeling victimized and helpless as a child, appearing as if a huge monster was holding her to eat her up but she could not get away.

She felt she could not get away because he kept saying he loved her, and he never said it otherwise. As a small child, she was confused between respecting her father's love and her own traumatic feelings at being manipulated for getting energies of sex and love which he could not get from her mother. He kept saying or feeling that nobody loves him but there was nothing in his behaviour which could lead to attracting love from another. He was abusive and alcoholic in his routine temperament.

She stared crying profusely with loud tears of fear and anger. The outburst of energy in water form was a release as this was the suppressed energy which had consciously converted into depression by being ignored. Just as a physical would develops septic by being ignored, an emotional wound increases in intensity if left unaddressed. I allowed her to release her suppressed depression by crying for some time. However, before the negative feelings could take charge of her being and increase her anger further, which could be self harming subsequently, I intervened and asked her to enter the scene as her adult self to help her the childhood self. The intention of healing is to reduce negative energy in the body and mind by integrating unattended soul fragments.

Lavanya was asked to enter as an adult and rescue the child. She took the child away from the ranting father. The father was taken by shock. He was reliving the sequence in spirit to extract love and positivity from her. Lavanya as an adult was directed to call the two white policemen and to throw light on the scene so that her father knows he is being watched. His ghost was made aware of his death. He was then forced to free the child. The energy cords of the child were cut with the spirit of the father so that the depression does not keep pulling her spirit in its grip. It is possible that the father's energy in her was confining her to depression by using her body to feel alive itself but was realistically, unable to live as he was already dead. The depression was akin to feelings of being dead residing in the body for the soul. That the father's spirit was trying to take over her body was apparent as she was being thrown off in the start of the session, as if prevented from entering her own body by a spirit. The spirit of the father was strong as the push she had felt had force in it. Electric violet flame has to be used only when the spirit is strong and evil as it is rigid about being the way it is, unwilling to change its selfish thinking.

The father was then sent to light and the black energy again electrocuted with electric violet flame. It takes repeated mind force to remove thee black energy. Lights were visualized onned in the house as a visualization of light spreading activates positive hormones in the body, thus, dispelling fear and darkness subconsciously.

The little 5 -year old child was cleansed by Lavanya as an adult to wash away the filthy, black energy of her father which covered her like dust. She was directed to take an energy shower of white light which washes the spirit's stored up energy like bathing. Her darkness and fear were subconsciously expelled by being washed away as dirty energy flowing out and being replaced by white/positive energy.

After the little girl was healed by the energy shower and made to realize that she was rescued from her father's manipulative molestation and was free to be herself; Lavanya was asked to apologize to the little child for leaving her unattended for so long and to promise her that she would never leave her again. She was then asked to integrate the child in her. The child was lighted up with bright energy and a smile. The same energies of relaxation filled up Lavanya's body.

The child's core filament of helplessness was thus systematically reversed so that she starts feeling strong again. The child now became a part of Lavanya's adult energy. Lavanya's aura was increased in size in alignment with allowing space for the integration.

While blocking away the evil energy, Lavanya screamed away her anger which she had been storing up against her father but had been unable to release as he had died abruptly. He released her frustration at her father for lying to her, as he had always pretended later that she had excessive sexual energy and he was afraid of her. Also, her mother had always made bad comments about the relationship between her and her father saying that sexual feelings were involved. She had felt extremely humiliated by her parents and felt sad because of their wrong blames and their bad behaviour. She confronted her parents and screamed out at them, thus releasing the suppressed anger and depression by confronting their actions.

The negative energy stored up in her mind was thus replaced with light. The spirits were made to give up their evil hold on her by showing them their own actions which were not indicative of a loving parenthood. She was directed to throw their energy out as sending out bad dolls so that she could free herself from the impact of their negativity on her mind. The father was sent away with his animal instincts with using the electric violent flame to dissolve his evil through the spirit release process

In her regular adult life, Lavanya always had a fear of being in the same rom as her father. Also, when she saw any old man holding hand of a little child, she felt tremors. The same type of tremor was seen in much greater intensity, as soon as she had entered the semi trance state.

She felt much lighter after releasing the fear of her father and his spirit from her energy self. This indicated that her subconscious self had been asking for healing since a long time. This exercise would create a dent in her energy of depression towards breaking the subconscious energy circuits moving in negative directions, which is necessary to slowly dissolve the depressed cloud on her head completely and replace it with energy of positive light on her head that would keep her healthy.

Fifth Inner Child Healing

After healing the 5-year-old, I asked Lavanya to move to any other situation where she had felt as abused. She started seeing herself at 13 when she was travelling with her parents. There was an uncle called Manmohan who was cheap in his usual behaviour with her. Her parents were having affairs outside the marriage with random people. They did not care about decent sexual conduct.

Lavanya said in the session "They know Manmohan Uncle was lewd. Even so, they asked me (the 13 year self) to sleep with him in the same room. "

Her face showed revulsion as she could see that he made sexual advances with her. She started crying as she felt totally helpless and miserable.

I asked her adult self to enter and help the child. Lavanya started crying loudly and screaming with anger at her parents. This release was necessary for her to remove their thoughts from her mind and respect her own body as clean.

I asked Lavanya to take the child away from the incestuous uncle. As an adult self, Lavanya had to tell the child that she was sorry she had abandoned her and that she would never leave her again. These words are necessary to help the child feel secure and trust her adult self.

Lavanya hugged the child and she voluntarily, asked her to change the dress to remove the filthy man's energy from herself. She was then directed to cut the child's cords with the uncle at all seven levels of chakra circuits.

Then she sent him away along with his animals. As remnants remained, she was again directed to throw out the uncle and put light on the place so that the darkness was dispelled, and the bad, negative spirits were made aware that their evil was watched...

The light destroyed the darkness and the hypocritical veil of goodness. The uncle and her parents were thrown away like dolls. The metaphor of dolls was used as dolls are insignificant. The dolls were thrown out of her house forcibly as they were not willing to leave on their own and were trying to suck away positive energy from her mind, by habit ... Her negative thinking about herself was partly due to the energy of her parents residing in her.

The 13 year old child was given an energy shower to remove the uncle's energy from her and she felt cleaned up. She was bathed, cleansed in spirit by Lavanya, hugged with warmth and sincerity, told that she loves her and will never leave her again. Then, the child smiled, and Lavanya integrated her inside her adult body. She was directed to see her aura two times her size as she integrated these two children in her.

Sixth Inner Child Healing

Next, she was asked to integrate herself as a baby girl who had been abused by her parents by negative comments passed unnecessarily. Lavanya had been called an ugly girl without reason repetitively by her parents. While compliments help a child develop self-esteem, criticism lowers the positive energy of the child. She needed to remove this belief from her mind from the core to regain her positive energy. I asked her to remove the energy of the comment and replace it with positive energy, hug the child, clean the child in energy shower to remove negative energy from her auric field and tell the child that she loves the child and would never leave the child again. Then, I asked her to sooth the chid till she smiles as a baby and then hug the child. She integrated the smiling baby in her.

I directed her to release the accumulated sadness and increase her positive energy by seeing her aura growing 4 times in size.

 As Lavanya grew up, her disagreements with her parents increased and her trust in their sincerity vanished. She saw her mother having affairs with different men and her father having an affair with her Mausi. There was no proper respectful conduct and there was lewd sexual conduct amongst the parents in front of the children. Her brother was being breast fed by her mother at 14. She also said that her mother tried to kiss her on the mouth when she was sleeping with her at 16. The mother was extremely abusive to her normally. She had suddenly awakened and left the bedroom in distaste.

First Inner Child Healing: Previous Session

Lavanya had healed three soul fragments of herself in her previous session in October 2018.

The first situation she healed was when she was about 4- 6 years old. She was being abused by her mother. She was rescued by Lavanya entering the situation and screaming at the other for misbehaving. The mother was told she has been watched by another adult and was not justified in her behaviour with the child. Her conduct was violently abusive and unhealthy for the child.

The child was taken away from the mother. Her energy cords were cut with her mother. The negative energy of the mother in her was released. Lavanya said sorry to the soul fragment that she had neglected her for so long and then gave her an energy shower to remove her sadness. Then, she took back her soul fragment from the mother and integrated it in herself.

Second Inner Child Healing

The next situation Lavanya saw was when she was 17. She was sitting in freezing cold weather in December in a cold place, as she had been locked outside the house by her mother. She had been found smoking and there had been some other disagreements with her mother. In anger, the mother had locked her outside.

When she was taken back in the house in the morning, she had taken high dosage of epilepsy tablets in anger and sadness. Then she was hospitalized for thirty days and she remembered nothing about that period. She was in coma.

Lavanya was directed in the session to enter as her bigger self and give a warm blanket to the child. Then, she was asked to make the mother forcibly open the door by entering as the police. The mother was extremely negative and unwilling to relent or regret. Hence, she was asked to burn her negative energy with electric violet light and cut cords with her.

While the child was given healing, she was crying and screaming at her mother. The anger was released by confronting her mother with adult help in the session. Then she was calmed down and given an energy shower of warmth and light. Her energy cords were cut again with the mother and her influence was removed from her mind. Once healed, calmed and de-freezed of feeling cold, the child was filled with positive energy and integrated in adult Lavanya.

Lavanya had been feeling excess cold in her present time also. This excessive feeling of cold should reduce after this healing once the anger and shock against the mother is sent away. Other than feeling less excessive cold, she would start feeling more confident and relaxed in everyday life.

Third Child Fragment Healing & Spirit Release

The third child fragment that Lavanya healed was the foetus of a baby. It appeared to be the baby she had aborted that may have been making her more suicidal. Lavanya had attempted suicide a few times since the abortion.

Lavanya had decided to abort the baby as it was created out of a sex episode which left her feeling violated and raped by a male friend. She had been married to someone else at that time. The sex had happened after a party where all of them had been drinking. There was an episode of crying and consoling which had turned violent. The man was beating her and making love to her. He did not understand the hideousness of the act. It happened once with him and never again. However, Lavanya had conceived. Her husband had agreed to keep the child. However, she decided that it was necessary to abort the child as it would remind her of the rape whenever she looked at it. She and her husband had divorced after the abortion.

Lavanya had taken her first session of hypnotherapy in 2006 to release the foetus and come to terms with it. She had looked relieved and integrated after the session as a major part of the foetus had been released. However, she had doubts. Also, a tiny fragment had remained which was probably stubbornly negative and did not want to let go. Lavanya later said that this could be her own energy from the time she was in the womb. Her mother had been wanting to abort her when she was in the womb but could not as the foetus was already six months old.

But, when she was seeing this energy in the session, she said "ITS NOT ME". It appeared to be the energy of another soul in her. Such energy transfer is natural after a pregnancy and abortion. Very often, aborted children remain as a part of the mother and grow in spirit.

Sometimes, they cause trauma in the mother, feelings of restlessness and sadness. The energy was very black. It was like a black, round, pulp ball. It had sadness and anger inside. It was given light to heal. Angels were called in this session to release the foetus again.

 Lavanya does not believe in angels and that doubt could block the release. Otherwise, angels are religiously conditioned into human minds as positive energies and would help a foetus reach God's light, if not obstructed by doubt. I asked Lavanya to just metaphorically visualize angels and send the foetus to light. The foetus took some time to dissolve its negativity and go into light.

Lavanya's cords with the rapist friend were also cut in the process so that this part of his energy could move out of her freely without any feelings of remorse or loyalty holding it back. The part of this foetus which was the spirit of Lavanya was taken back in her body and integrated as an inner child fragment.

Lavanya's suicidal needs may subside after these sessions though other factors can influence.

The soul fragments of the energy of Lavanya was integrated and her aura was brightened. Her cords with her mother were cut again and the mother's influence was removed as energy release from her being. She could let go of the mother's beliefs subsequently and be her own self in her self talk. As the mother was unnecessarily abusive, critical and incestuous due to her megalomania bipolar disorder, this release was necessary to get free of insane, impulsive, self-harming behaviour.

Conclusive Interpretation

Lavanya's first session had involuntarily led to the release of her mother's dominance over her subconscious energy.

Her next session led to the release of the dominance of her father over her subconsciously including a spirit release. A dead spirit can create symptoms of depression in the body as it is dead but wants to stay alive. Depression is felt as death by the subconscious mind as it involves a lowering of souls revolving frequency.

The release of the father's spirit should reduce feelings of imbalance in her including reducing of alcohol, as her father was an alcoholic.

The release of mother and father involved the use of electric violet flame which acts like a laser beam when stubborn spirits refuse to release their energy otherwise.

Her father's release and the release of feelings of molestation was necessary for Lavanya to feel clean within herself and attract other energies to herself which were clean intentionally.

Further Suggestions

:for preventing a collapse, depression attack or suicidal thoughts

Lavanya has to understand that several of her thoughts about herself maybe coming from her mother or father and she has to release these negative thoughts with awareness that they not her own rational thoughts .In her own sensibility, she would not commit suicide but the travelling thought waves from her mother who wanted to abort her or her father's spirit, who is dead may want her to kill herself.

Lavanya's parents were highly successful people in powerful positions when they retired. Hence, respecting their intellect was natural but their thoughts came with ingrained darkness.

All thoughts are composed of energies as is explained at length in my book:

'CREATION OF HAPPINESS: THE ENERGY WAR, a soul's perspective'. Thoughts travel in thought waves and can enter your mind as sound waves or light waves do. Hence, you have to heal your inner radio frequency to remove all negative feelings as energies as they otherwise, lower your soul frequency; thus, creating restlessness, depression etc. in the body.

Medicines of depression create positive hormones and can help realistically, only if your inner creation of negative hormones by focusing on negative thinking (From the present or past) is not involuntarily higher than the release of positive hormones by the medicines. If you are constantly focusing on feelings of anger or helplessness whether in self or in others, you would emit negative hormones on a persistent basis which would over rule production of any positive hormones by medicines. Instead doing self-healing therapies to release negativity from the mind as energies and fuelling the mind to deliberately focus on positive feelings leads to cutting on involuntary negative energy circuits. With awareness, it is possible to focus on positive feelings by choice and detach from negative feelings about self and others, without alcohol and without drugs.

 The idea of healing should be to test yourself and check on your frequency. If you are feeling negative, check your thoughts and detach from all negative feelings. Take time to be alone for two hours with music, without alcohol ad without weeds. Just be breathing or focusing on the top of your head, focus on a smile or any pleasant imagination or exhale lying down as in sleeping, without guilt. Just being with your energy would make you release energies others and uplift your current to a positive focus, which is necessary to now allow drowning into negative thought currents. Healing is all about activating mind force to get to a state where you can uplift yourself. Some more sessions maybe required to attain the strength to uplift the inner self.

Daily meditation

1. Focus on the top of your head for one minute, exhale out black smoke and inhale white light.

2. Smile for a minute. Smiling activates release of positive hormones to organs.
3. Focus on the centre of your forehead and your chest. Exhale black smoke and inhale white light.
4. Count ten good things about yourself every day to increase fuel on maintaining the good.
5. You can throw away 5 bad things about yourself every day in an imagined dustbin and ask it to dissolve.
6. Count ten good things you like about your work. Throw away five negative feelings. Keep the throwing away lesser than the adding up to maintain a positive average balance of power as negative energy also gives you life force power.
7. Keep feet in water daily to uncoil. Put salt once a week if negative energy feels heavy as n depression or exhaustion.
8. Take two hours for yourself or at least eleven or twenty minutes where you just be
9. Sleep 8 hours every day.
10. Focus your eyes upwards to prevent depression. If you don't get sleep, stay on bed doing nothing with focus on your head. You can also Rotate your eyes left to right and bottom to top to release angry memories. These are short cut methods which would work where deep healing is not required.
11. Take weekly off.
12. Keep cutting energy cords with all places of tension and people who drain you out. Take your power back and give their soul energy in you back to them as you will not make their choice.

13. Reward yourself whenever you do or think
    something good before waiting for
    acknowledgement from others.
14. Keep saying "I like Myself; I like my work, Thank you
    Earth."
15. Say I LOVE MYSELF daily and exhale all energies out
    which disagree. Cut cords with your parents again
    and again if there is too much resistance from within.

Appendix 1

A Summary of the Case History

- A summary of the detailed case history is given here :

- Lavanya (name changed) aged 40.5 years, wanted a hypnotherapy session to relax. She had been diagnosed for clinical depression. She had overused the medication, Valium, and had been hospitalized with coma for four days. Hence, she said she needed alternative methods to relax.

She was taken into semi –hypnosis through 7 successive induction methods till she reached a calm state in her body language. Then, she was asked to lie down and focus on the inside of her body while imagining for the duration of the session, that the outside world did not exist. Once she allowed herself to be calm and semi-drowsy, she voluntarily saw memories on incest and abuse as a small child by her parents. She cried profusely in the session and underwent a release of suppressed emotion. She was given suggestions to release the memory pictorially and accept freedom from traumatic memories in her subconscious mind. She felt much more relaxed and balanced after the session.

This release of depressed energy was facilitated by the process of slowing down the brain which facilitated a review of the inner self. This kind of involuntary release could not have been experienced without reducing the brain frequency from beta to alpha levels.

Thus, clinical hypnosis helps in treatment of suppressed emotions as psychoanalysis does. By complementing it with regular breathing exercises and behavioural healing methods, it helps in facilitating speedy and long term healing of emotional or physical diseases. By adding hypnotic healing methods, side effects of medicines are minimized and results are more easily visible,

APPENDiX 2- DISCLAIMER 1

Hypnosis, psychotherapy, NLP or any meditation practice is not against using medicines. These are deeper methods of healing the inner body mechanism which creates problems on the surface. Medical treatment or using aggressive methods to self-heal anger, come into play once problems come on the surface but positive thinking can be cultivated from childhood so that problems are released by change in thinking patterns to be more progressive over traditional..

Spirituality says that medical help needs to be complemented with mind training to stay positive once the problem is resolved or the problems will return till the root cause is addressed in the subconscious mind. Positive thinking increases by using self hypnosis and emotional management methods like NLP and psychotherapy.

Taking allopathic treatment using science or using anger as a sword shifts onus of the problem to outside the self, thus passing your powers as the co-creator to another energy which may or may not be in agreement with your karmic decisions. The need for revenge takes you away from pursuing justice.

Just fuming, crying or taking medicines will not solve any problem in the long term. External treatment will increase sleepiness, depression or aggression depending on whether you habitually use fight or flight syndrome by your primitive mind-set conditioning.

Fighting wars to get justice or using medicines help to cleanse a mess which has surfaced up ,but do not heal the causes which create the mess. The cause is not just external chemical imbalance but also negative thinking in the subconscious mind which has to be uplifted to positive by using therapeutic methods which address the individual's subconscious mind.

At a deeper level, the disease, corruption or terrorism, are a reflection of problems in society and the imbalance needs to be cleared by cleansing the mass thinking of society to be less hypocritical in orientation and more meaningfulness oriented. with progress being the goal over stagnating traditional roles.

Appendix 3- Disclaimer 2

The name and identity of the person has been changed while keeping he broader parameters similar, to maintain professional privacy while facilitating research.

This case history has been chosen as it could directly be categorized under the label of depression. Though I have several case history reports, I have not yet written a book on past life therapy which would cover several examples of cases in different spheres of trauma and their sudden healing, catharsis or realizations. Maybe I will write those later.

The client permissions are asked for before publishing a case history, either verbally or through email. Some people refuse. The person whose case history is published receives good karma and his healing or soul evolution is empowered such that s/he is overtime led to find satisfaction with his or her choices. Publishing of a case history can be part of a soul contract where large scale karmic healing is required to heal the karmic debt of the spirit.

All case histories are not written in books. Only those are published which can explain a phenomenon through a perspective which has not been widely published before to facilitate healing of several through a similar method or which can create a change in society eg. by making people realize that hypocrisy harms , this case history can motivate a subtle positive change in behaviour of some people who maybe incestuous when non guarded with ethical morality..

Unlike medication or magic, hypnosis cannot be applied to heal any person external to the self who is unwilling to receive the healing. Hypnosis can be used as Remote Healing or Distance healing but only with willing participation from the person himself or herself to do the mental exercises later. Every session has follow up exercises which have to be taken as medicines after surgery for the effects of the session to sink in and be maintained by the body. The exercises recommended appear simple but use focused energy resources of the mind. Hypnosis does not usually help if the client expects automatic healing without any effort on part of the self.

APPENDIX 4 – SELF HELP SCRIPT OF SELF HYPNOSIS

1. Sit in a chair in a relaxed position, spine straight but relaxed, feet flat on floor.

- Keep both hands open, fingers spread out. Place hands on thighs.

- Relax your facial muscles and your shoulders.

- Feel balanced in your body posture. Be comfortable and in control. Know that you are safe. The process will not mesmerize you. It will only help you relax and be focused.

- Now, keep your chin parallel to the ground.

- While keeping your chin parallel to the ground, bring your eyes down and begin to watch both your hands simultaneously.

- Keep on watching both hands for some time - maintaining focus on both hands.

- Also, be aware of your incoming breath and outgoing breath.

- In case your eyes feel tired, you can close your eyes while maintaining awareness of the two points and your breathing. You can wake yourself up by letting go.

2. Going deeper:
3. In case you lose focus, bring it back as soon as you are aware that you have lost focus. Be in this state for a few seconds.

- Going deeper - Now, start counting backwards from 25-1. At 1, you are in a deep level of your subconscious mind. Take a deep breath; exhale and say RELAX to yourself. Allow yourself to be in a relaxed state of mind now.
- Maintain this detached State of Zero thinking before starting work on the healing cycle in your subconscious. Be in this state of mental quietness for a second or five seconds. (It is also called a gap or *brake* state as it puts a brake on negative thinking.)

4. You are focused on both your hands and your breath, simultaneously so that your mind is blank of any repetitive worries.
5. Now, think of a persistent nagging negative memory. Start accessing that memory as described in detail.
6. See the memory as if happening now. Clearly visualize the colours of the picture.
7. Hear the sound
8. Feel the feelings, which came about.
9. Hear your own talk to yourself and to others.
10. After you have visualized the memory, erase it .

11. For erasing the memory, blur the visions from coloured to black & white, reduce the sounds and mute them or hear donkeys wailing in their place, make the film hazy, allow it to shake and blur, rewind it and move it forward, keep shaking it up till its hold loses in your mind and then erase it by imagining light falling on it.

12. Again if it comes up ,keep reducing its intensity and recreate a picture you like as you desire with the same intensity .Hear the sounds, see the picture, feel the emotions of control in you.

13. Then, after you have both the pictures, once again visualize the old picture ad feel it less intensely than the new picture where you are happier and more in control. Now, again erase the old film and see the new film taking over its place. Feel negative energy from the old film going into Earth or the ocean and dissolving into a positive formless state as by getting mixed up in or water.

14. Now, after you have the desired picture in front of you, make it as big as you can and absorb it in you.

15. Then, ground yourself into Earth by imagining yourself as a big tree going deep into Earth.

16. Thank Earth, Thank God or your Life force, thank your body and your mind for co-operating with your dreams.

17. Also, you may thank the energies who have left you so that they could be free of punishing you and you could be free of traumas required to complete your dreams.

18. Count yourself up from 1 to 25 to be back in your normal state of mind.
19. Feel integrated with your conscious mind. Tell yourself "I am integrated and relaxed. Thanks"
20. Think of a positive lesson you learnt from the trauma. If nothing comes up immediately, think of the positive lesson as white light entering you. Receive the lesson you learnt from the trauma as an energy or words or thoughts and store it as white light inside you .
21. Release the old sad film in air and cut your cords with it as cutting the string of a kite. See yourself coming back in your own body from the film with the learning as white light to a piece of white paper. Integrate yourself in your body on Earth with the white light
22. Smile and feel complete for a moment and refresh yourself if needed by doing some stretching exercises.

Appendix 5 - 22 Strategies for Replacing Depression with Soul Ascension

A few do's and dont's to overcome depression which can be followed are:

Do This:

1. *Independent thinking over obedience cult. Detaching from blind imitation of fashionable success trends by reducing dependence on others' thinking & learning to connect to your own inner self by meditation, self – healing, therapy etc. to understand your needs of satisfaction.*
2. *Taking action for pursuit of inner satisfaction over maintaining a superficial good image of happiness. Understanding the difference between glitter and gold, body & soul as body adoration or dissatisfaction in relationships or work can lead to depression.*
3. *Confrontation of your own needs and understanding the self over hiding behind curtains of survival, morality, self -deception or hypocrisy.*

4.   *Meditating in complete silence with focus on breathing while imagining a light beaming in your stomach, head & feet to recharge your life force.*

5.   *Understanding the ZERO STATE of being as a transition between a negative thought state and a positive thought state. Zero state is a phase of being thoughtless which can last from a few seconds to a minute. Practising being thoughtless for being in a zero state to move to being positive , which has to be done with deliberate effort akin to applying a brake in a moving car as being thoughtless applies a brake on moving circuits of negative thinking.*

6.   *Looking up more than looking downwards as looking upwards helps you stay thoughtless and thus prevents negative thinking.*

7.   *Using self talk to speak the opposite of your negative thoughts to yourself to energize positive thinking and feelings of being positive. Eg. Say 'I appreciate my work' instead of saying ' Nobody likes my work'*

8.   *Using visual imagination to think of happy moments which you would like to feel in the future instead of allowing the negative to occur automatically as an outcome of current neural circuits of negative thinking@ Learning to Dissociate from worrying, Apply brakes on thoughts, Think Positive, Reverse Direction of Inner filament , Be Positive automatically over a period of time.*

9.   *Staying connected to your creative nature's side by doing some activity which does not pay you with good marks, praise or money like gardening, cooking*

, painting , dancing, singing, swimming, writing, cleaning etc.

10. *Search for Love over temporary satisfaction with Lust , by starting the shift to being positive with loving and liking yourself at the core.*

11. *Self- controlling Id impulses - Tantric self -stimulation or using masturbation with orgasmic release of energy by taking It up from the root chakra with a forceful breath and releasing it from the crown chakra in the head . The same exercise can be done by simply breathing up from the bottom of the spinal cord and releasing the breath from the top of the head, approximately 3 times and breathing back into the centre of the chest or the heart chakra. This energy upliftment exercise helps to increase creative life force energy overflow in the brain, over aimless masturbation, watching porn or prostitution. As a side effect, this exercise improves internal balance, intelligence and creative thinking.*

12. *Deliberately creating positive self- talk over blaming the self or others or society.*

13. *Using peaceful methods for mental release of trauma over aggression ;like cognitive behaviour therapy, reading self –help books, deep breathing exercises, erasing sad memories through emotional management, self –hypnosis for relaxation , spirit release for improvements in health etc.*

14. *Indulging in preparing food for yourself over eating junk by allowing feelings of being light & healthy to rule your intuition while preparing food over eating just for dieting or fashion.*

15. Increasing Water intake as a substitute for alcohol or drugs to maintain internal hormonal balance.
16. Taking out time to be thoughtless to calm nerves, instead of taking out time to smoke a cigarette which creates the same effect as thoughtlessness to calm nerves but has side effects.
17. Choosing to sleep more to be free from pressure over accentuating internal drama . Avoid watching television and sit idle watching a still picture or listen to chants, music etc. to claim inner free space till you get enough rest or calmness to feel stress free, refreshed mentally and healthy.
18. Using deep breathing exercise, walking and smiling meditation at least 22 minutes daily.
19. Taking time for recharging yourself along with positive thinking over constantly working to meet demands of good performance or social prestige.

The Dont's – DO NOT THINK ThESE to AVOID DEPRESSON

1. Do not think money is the most important priority of life and you have to drown in sadness to save your money or your family's money/respect..
2. Do not think others are perfect and you are inferior just because they fit conventionally in society's standards of success.
3. Do not think success brings happiness automatically without positive thinking .
4. Do not think God can help you by giving you positive energy without you making efforts to uplift your

positive vibrational frequency to receive or maintain positive tuning.

5. *Avoid sex with strangers .Do not believe sex is purely physical and will not affect your mental intelligence or emotional energies. Sex causes a DNA energy exchange and karmic imprints on energies. You may catch a negative person's sadness just because you have had sex with him or her and be unable to shake it off. Feeling sad will fog your brain and hence, lower your ability to use your intelligence. Energy is transmitted as a virus and you will need to actively heal your energies to be positive again and again if you continue the relationship.*

A one -time sexual affair will also leave an impact on your subconscious which you will have to erase to heal yourself back to being positive by overcoming the trauma, while imbibing the learning which every difficulty entails.

.

Please refer to my book EMOTIONAL ENERGY MANAGEMENT for more details on emotional healing for improvements in health and happiness.

Acknowledgements

- Master Practitioner of Neuro Linguistic Programming ,2007. American Board For NLP.
- Certificate in Applied Behaviour Analysis & Managing Uncontrollable Behaviours, Parent Training Programs, USA,2002
- Certificate in Advanced DNA 2 Theta Healing , Japan,2007.
- Reiki Master Training , Muscat & Australia,2004
- Psychology, Robert.A.Baron. 2011, published by Pearson , fifth edition ,2002.Master's Degree in Psychology.
- Kaplan and Sadock's Synopsis of Psychiatry, 11th edition, published by Wolters Kluwer India, Pvt. Ltd. 2014
- Workshops on Life Transformation and Deep Healing by Rd. Hans Ten dam, TASSO Instituut, Holland,2006-2008
- Diploma in Clinical Hypnotherapy conducted by Dr. Sunny Satin, California Hypnosis Institute, endorsed by American Hypnosis Association,2005-2

o Advanced workshop on Past Life therapy, by Maggie van Staveren, IAART, 2nd World Congress on Regression and Past life Therapy, New Delhi, India

o On-line parent training certificate programmed in Applied Behaviour Analysis conducted by Behaviour Analysts, INC. USA.

o A course in Vipassana meditation

Books

- 'The Destiny of Souls' by Michael Newton, Ph.D., published by Llewellyn Worldwide, 2006.
- 'What We May Be' by Pierre Ferruco, published by Jeremy P. Tarcher, INC., Los Angeles, 1982
- ' The Tao of Physics' by Frito Capra,by Flamingo, Harper Collins Publishers, London, 1991
- 'Only Love is Real' by Dr. Brian Weiss, published by Piatkus Books Limited, UK, 2006
- 'Taking Learning to Task', by Jane Vella, published by Jossey Bass,San Francisco, 2001
- 'Essential Energy Balancing' by Diane Stein, published by Crossing Press , Toronto, 2000
- 'The Science of Psychic Surgery' by Benjamin. O. Bibb and Joseph. .J. Weed
- 'Know How' by Leslie Cameron Bandler, David Gordon ,Michael Lebeau, published by Real People Press, Utah,1985
- ' Lost in Space' by Mike Dooley, published by Totally Unique Thoughts, USA,1998
- 'Taking Learning to Task', by Jane Vella, published by Jossey Bass,San Francisco, 2001
- 'Essential Energy Balancing' by Diane Stein, published by Crossing Press , Toronto, 2000
- 'The Science of Psychic Surgery' by Benjamin. O. Bibb and Joseph. .J. Weed
- ' Illusions' by Richard Bach, published by Arrow Books, London, 1998
- 'How Psychic are you?' by Julie Soskin, published by the Penguin Group, USA, 2002

ABOUT THE AUTHOR

Dr. Shiva Swati @ Swati Rao Shiv, CCht. RMP (A.M.) is an Energy healer, Soul Empowerment Guru and Emotional Management therapist. She specializes in healing emotional or physical problems with unknown causes. She has been practicing hypnotherapy, pranik healing, NLP, spirit release, life between life counseling, reiki and past life therapy for several years. Her work focuses on teaching happiness as a mind discipline while helping clients ascend their souls through healing physical diseases like asthma, diabetes, spondylitis etc. , relationship conflicts, confidence problems, removal of phobias, negative spirit attachments etc.

She works for light and channels a rainbow soul. In her free time, she meditates intensively and downloads information in silent conversations with cosmic light. Her passion is to be one with God. The purpose of her soul is to help change the educational structure of the world so that everyone feels free to be happy, in peace and healthy, as an outcome of a conditioned habit to focus on positive feelings, from childhood. She is a part of an ascended, multi-dimensional soul, working for upliftment of human consciousness to a higher positive frequency in tune with cosmic awakening energy of the NEW AGE.

For any queries, you can contact the author at:

rswaati@yahoo.com
Dr. Shiva Swati,
RMP (A.M)
Certified Clinical Hypnotherapist, Past Life Regression Therapist, Life between Life therapist, Master NLP Practitioner, Time Line Therapist, Spirit Release Therapist, Reiki Master, Advanced Pranik Healer, DNA2 Theta Healer, Behaviour Analyst

Sahyog apartments, Mayur Vihar 1, Delhi 91, INDIA
E mail –shivaswaati.voiceofgod@gmail.com

www.shivaswati.com

www.ingramcontent.com/pod-product-compliance
Lightning Source LLC
Chambersburg PA
CBHW051230250726
48655CB00006B/2687